Michigan and the War of 1812

By

George P. Watt, Jr., MAOM, MMH

Thank you Gary for
reading my book!!
You're a great Friend.
God Bless you.
your friend in
christ,
George P. Watt

Acknowledgements

I want to first acknowledge my Capstone Advisor for this project, Dr. John Broom. He was instrumental in keeping me focused and was very patient with my many errors going through this process. I also want to acknowledge my fellow Norwich students who earned their Master Degree in Military History in 2007 alongside me. I want to acknowledge my friends, family and all history enthusiasts who love history as much as me. Most importantly I want to thank my Lord and Savior Jesus Christ for his strength to endure life and the many struggles that has occurred.

Watt

Abstract

The Michigan Territory saw a number of engagements during the War of 1812. The British and American military saw the Michigan Territory as a strategic position which had an economic benefit through the fur trade. The Michigan Territory was the staging ground for one element of an American invasion of Canada. The Battle of the River Raisin in the Michigan Territory was an inspiration for American military forces during the duration of the war.

Watt

Table of Contents

Introduction

Watt

The Michigan Territory was a vital area for the War of 1812 because of its location on the Great Lakes, can this be proven? Why was the Michigan Territory so important to the United States and Great Britain? Were there any major battles in Michigan? Did an invasion occur from any part of Michigan into Canada? How did the British take the coastal fortifications in the Michigan Territory so easily? Was Fort Michilimackinac and Fort Mackinac the same fort? What was the location of this fort? Were Regular military units better than Militia units in battle? These are questions that must be answered in order to evaluate Michigan's role in the War of 1812.

The Northwest Territories had an economic benefit prior to the War of 1812 for both the United States and Great Britain. The Michigan Territory was part of the fur trade industry. In fact, "Chicago and Michilimackinac were strategic areas for the fur trade."[1] An example of how important the fur trade was to this area is with the boundaries that were set. "The British company, Northwest Fur Company, agreed to operate within specific areas of the United States, specifically the Michigan Territory, but were also given stock in the newly formed United States company, Southwest

Watt

Fur Trade Company."[2]   These land boundaries and sharing of stock

in the newly formed fur trading company shows how important the

Michigan territory was to everyone involved. This economic benefit

and Michigan's strategic location on the Great Lakes made it a

perfect target for Great Britain.[3]

Prior to 1763, the French owned the Michigan Territory. The

French surrendered it to Great Britain at the conclusion of the French

and Indian War in 1763. Great Britain gave the newly formed

United States the Northwest Territory including the Michigan

Territory in 1783. Michigan became a separate territory for the

United States in 1805 and William Hull was appointed its first

Governor.[4] This was prior to the War of 1812 when military

tensions were becoming evident with Great Britain. This also

happened as heightening tensions and fighting with Native

Americans had been occurring. Hull's first responsibility was to

create a strategic plan of action in case there was war with Britain.

Hull's plan would include "reinforcing Detroit with regular infantry

units, create a Great Lakes naval force and create roads as a means

of troop movement." [5]

Hull's strategy was a direct result of American strategic philosophies which included the use of a militia system and coastal fortifications. The United States also began to rely on its navy. The strategic idea of a militia system can be traced to American's feared a centralized government controlling the military. This forced American military leaders to rely on a militia system. The need to "provide and maintain a navy" was also instilled into the American military strategy.[6] Both the militia system and the creation of a naval force were required by the United States Constitution. American military strategy also required the reinforcement of costal fortification for the protection of harbor cities.[7]

Unlike the American military, the British used a strong standing army which was trained, disciplined and would fight in tight linear formations in battle. The British were willing to ally with Native American tribes who did not like the American settlers on their land. The British also had the stronger navy during the War of 1812. This form of warfare required discipline and training as keys to battle, but it also was a direct result of the military technologies. Artillery was an important part of this type of warfare.

Watt

Firearms required training to provide accuracy in battle. The British

military were well trained because of their involvement with the

Napoleonic wars. Initially, this was an advantage to the American

military because the British were fighting the French. As the British

cycled units into Canada, their experience would start to show on the

battlefield.[8]

The Michigan Territory saw a number of military

engagements during the War of 1812. Some of these were minor or

without blood, such as with the loss of Fort Michilimackinac on

Mackinac Island and Hull's surrender at Fort Detroit. There is one

battle that did give inspiration for the duration of the war and that

was the Battle of River Raisin otherwise known as the Battle of

Frenchtown.[9] The River Raisin was important for many reasons. It

proves the importance of the Michigan Territory for the British as a

means of gaining strategic position against the American military.

It shows the tension between Native American tribes and the

American military. One of the biggest aspects of the battle was its

inspirational motivation for the second American invasion of

Canada.[10] The battle cry of, "Remember the Raisin!" would be

heard for the duration of the war.[11]

The Michigan Territory also saw the American military launch one element of the invasion of Canada. American political leaders had hopes of gaining Canada as part of the United States. The first invasion would initially be affected by the losses of Fort Michilimackinac and they eventually forced a retreat back into Fort Detroit. This setback would give the British an advantage but as the American forces regrouped, they would launch a second and successful invasion of Canada. This second invasion would see the American military regain lost territory in Michigan and conquer new territories in Canada.[12]

Michigan's role in the War of 1812 is solidified with the various battles that occurred. Economic gain also swayed military warfare in the area. The Northwest Fur Company would push for the attack and conquest of Fort Michilimackinac. This meant they would refit their merchant ships as military vessels. The American military also saw Canada as an opportunity for military gain. Both sides saw the strategic and economic advantages of the Michigan Territory and Great Lakes.[13] The various strategies that were seen in the territory foster the idea of a Western Way of War.[14]

Western Warfare and the War of 1812

Watt

The Western Way of War thesis was created by Victor Hanson which traces western warfare back to ancient warriors such as the Greeks. This style of warfare can be viewed from specific categories. This "economic and political hegemony of the West" is a key factor when evaluating western warfare including the War of 1812.[15] The west allocated its natural and economic resources to the military for the creation of new technologies for war. Another key aspect of Hanson's Western Way of War is "civic militarism."[16] This "civic militarism" plays right into American practices of a militia system.[17] The militia system involved a number of variables beyond this idea.[18]

Western warfare involves the interrelationship between the military and political goals.[19] There is a direct relationship with this idea in the War of 1812. Political events occurred which required some form of diplomatic and military action. This involved the military as the means of obtaining the best chances for victory. Political issues with Great Britain and the treatment of American sailors was an important issue for American political leaders. The United States was becoming a role player in commerce. In fact the unsuccessful invasion of Canada stemmed from political motives.

There are a number of conflicting views concerning the causes of war. Historians also disagree about the causes of the war with this said, common themes can be found.[20]

Some key themes were the impressments of American sailors. A second theme was the "Chesapeake Affair."[21] A third theme was British "restrictions on free or neutral trade."[22] A forth theme was laws restricting American trade which restricted American goods in British held territories. Each theme alone cannot explain America's willingness to fight Great Britain; however, together they have credence. The most popular theme is the impressments of American soldiers. This theme did occur as a direct result of Great Britain being involved with the Napoleonic Wars and the need for sailors. The clarification must be made with who was being impressed by the British. It was former British subjects that had become American citizens. One of the biggest issues resulted from the British mistakenly taking naturalized Americans as British subjects thus taking American citizens.[23]

The first theme was impressments of Americans which can be estimated at approximately "three thousand to ten thousand Americans."[24] This became an immediate issue. America was in a tough situation. The British held the seaways which American merchant ships traveled thus the interaction was inevitable. The British were in an equally tough situation because of the Napoleonic wars. This however does not give way to the British policy because one nation should not be able to force another nation's citizens into military service. Sailor shortages in the Royal Navy created this need for the impressments of American sailors. Donald R. Hickey points out that it was a price that Americans needed to accept for doing business with a "world at war."[25] The fact is that this British policy affected American national rights in the world.[26]

The second theme of "The Chesapeake Affair" was an incident where the British enforced its strategic position which was to impress its subjects off American ships.[27] This is because American military ships were a safe haven for British sailors who deserted, however in this case, the British attempted to board and when refused fired upon the Chesapeake killing American sailors. Although the British agreed it was in the wrong and would offer settlement to victims, it could not come to an agreement with American politicians to end impressment. This created greater tensions between the United States and Great Britain.[28]

Watt

The third theme was not allowing free trade with nations, specifically the French. The British believed the United States were aiding the French war effort against the British thus believed it was acceptable to disallow any neutral country from trading with France. The Napoleonic Wars dominated world politics and this issue was no exception. This "Orders in Council" gave the British Navy an opportunity to take American merchant ships and property if believed to be heading for any French controlled port. Hickey again points out that this British policy was a direct result of the Napoleonic Wars; however this would mean a country cannot stay neutral in times of war. It must be pointed out that a neutral country and its citizens have the right to trade with whomever they want, even in times of war.[29]

The final theme was a series of laws that prohibited American merchants from trading with British held territories. These laws by American lawmakers were an attempt to relate economic need of foreign nations and American diplomacy. The goal of these laws was to limit British prosperity in North America. Although the laws can be traced as a means to detour the British War effort, most of it was economical in nature. Some of these policies effect America's freedom in the world. Hickey's cost of doing business theory may be true, but it also must be stated that a neutral country can declare war from these acts being committed.[30]

Declaring war and fighting a war are separate issues for political and military leaders. Fighting a war has many aspects. The British and Americans used similar tactics; however the British strong standing army was better for this from of warfare. The British tactic was to put their soldiers into "battalions which were well organized."[31] These units would march in columns creating linear formations on the battlefield.[32] American warfare was based on coastal fortifications, a militia system and a gunboat policy.[33] This explains the American military's lack of readiness for the War of 1812, in contrast to the British's policy that was well defined.[34]

British Military Strategies and Tactics

The British had a strong standing army and the most powerful navy in the world. The British were battle ready because of the fighting in Europe. The British military had the best military technologies in the world. Their military leaders created a number of tactics starting with the formation of the units. This formation would create two linear columns on the battlefield. The width of the formation would depend on the topographical aspect of the terrain.

The British placed importance on training and discipline. This can

be seen on the battlefield with the tight formations and the ability of

the soldiers to fire rapidly during the battle. [35]

The British had regular military and naval units stationed in

Canada; however, they would form citizen militia units of Canadians

alongside their military. The British would use forty thousand

troops by the end of the war.[36] This was an important part of British

military strategy which was strength in numbers. The British also

used Native American tribes as a viable force. The British

understood that Native Americans were unhappy with the amount of

Americans that were settling their territories in the Northwest.[37]

The British would use this tension against America to their

advantage. A member of the House of Lords in the British

Parliament justified the use of Native American tribes and stated,

"The British had every right to use any means which God and Nature

had given them."[38] They would allow the Native Americans to use

their strengths as fearless warriors in battle. An example of this can

be read from the diaries of John Robison who was a sixteen year old

British enlistee.[39] Robison wrote that he remembered "vividly the march to Brownstown."[40] He describes the Native American

warriors when he wrote, "the troops interrupted the solitude of the

scene, rendered more imposing by the wild appearance of warriors,

whose bodies, stained and painted in the most fearful manner."[41]

Another aspect of British strength was their navy. In 1812,

"the British Navy had around 600 fighting ships."[42] The British

ships were better equipped, gunned and manned compared to the

United States Navy. American merchants had also relied on the

British to keep peace in the Atlantic Ocean and Mediterranean Sea

and the ports along the European and African continents. In fact, the

"Royal Navy held balance in naval power in the Atlantic until the

end of the age of sails."[43] This was a direct result of American

strategic policy which had a more defensive mindset. Although

Congress authorized ships, they did not compare in number to the

British Navy. The British military relied on its naval strength.[44]

The strength of the British Navy was the ability to destroy its

enemies. During the Napoleonic wars, the British Navy defeated the

French on a number of occasions and became the mistress of the

seas. The ability of the British to defeat the French Navy shows the

strength of the British Navy. These sailing ships would fight in a line or in single action side by side to the enemy ship but this was an open sea strategy. An equal strategy was creating a blockade of the enemy's ports. This strategy was one that worked well for the stronger British Navy against American ports. The British cabinet commented that it would use this strategy, "Haste the Americans into submission."[45] This was a significant challenge for any American military strategist.[46]

American Military Strategies

American strategy relied on a militia system and coastal fortifications. The goal of political leaders was to revamp the coastal fortifications from the Revolutionary era. The militia system realized the idea of having a few true military units and the creation of new units relied on calling up the average citizen as part of its military force. This was great for defensive warfare but not for offensive action like President Madison wanted. The naval strategy was that of a "gun boat strategy."[47] America military strategic situation was made worse because of the "Jeffersonian defensive strategy."[48] American warfare was also formed from fighting with Native American tribes.[49]

American political leaders had hoped to defeat Great Britain with diplomatic polices backed by military force however Great Britain was the best military force in the world at this time. The only true rival was Napoleon. The United States Navy was meager at best. It had a few ships which had performed well during the Barbary Wars, but this was no comparison to what the British Navy had accomplished during this time period. Although justified, America was not prepared for war with Great Britain. Logistics was another issue for American military leaders.[50]

Diplomacy failed to stop war and misconceptions about the Canadian population becoming part of the United States was another problem. America's opinion was that the, "British must be forever driven from all their possessions in North America."[51] American political leaders had hoped for a quick invasion of Canada with the idea that Canadians would rise up against the British and join the American fight. Political leaders had believed that Canadians wanted to be part of the United States. In reality, Canadians feared American encroachment because of the number of United States citizens that had moved into Canada along the American border. This created tensions with Canada and the United States.[52]

Watt

Unlimited Warfare

Unlimited warfare came to America from the colonists that settled in the area. This form of military strategy was part of a broader European strategy of the time. Unlimited warfare would be a strategy of annihilation on any military or civilian population the offensive military attacked. The frontier life and continuous fighting with Native American tribes embedded this concept as a main strategy in America. This form of fighting would lead to the formation of Ranger units in the colonies. Ranger units would roam the frontier as an offensive weapon against Native Americans. This would include scalping and other gruesome acts of fighting. These Ranger units would create unlimited warfare on the frontier and this would carry over to future military strategies in frontier territories.[53]

Ranger units would see action through the War of 1812. In the Northwest Territory, Native American tribes started fighting back. This forced American military leaders to take action against them. One form of warfare was "search and destroy" missions against Native Americans which fostered their relationship with the British as the War of 1812 came to fruition. Indiana's Territorial Governor William Benjamin Harrison would write of, "avenging his country and saving the frontier."[54] These search and destroy actions in the Northwest Territory became part of the American military strategy during the War of 1812.[55]

The British would see the use of unlimited warfare and Ranger units too. During the fighting with the Irish in Ireland and during the Jacobite Rebelling in Scotland, the British military unleashed fury on these enemies without remorse. During the French and Indian War, the British would see the need for the Ranger units. The British initially did not like the idea of Ranger units, typically these units lacked discipline. They would eventually see the need for them. These Ranger units would incorporate Native American tribes as part of its fighting force. This was an example of how the British would use Native American allies in battle.[56]

Militia System

The United States Constitution called for a militia system. This would be the primary source of soldiers for the new republic. The creation of a standing army was controlled and limited because the fear of a strong central government. This stemmed from the past dealing with the British governmental system. The trust in a militia system was a direct result of "America's fear of a standing army."[57]

Watt

The militia system was based on the premise that the average citizen could be called up in a moment's notice in order to form a military unit. This strategy was another example of the United States creating a military of defense. This was the premise of the Jeffersonian military strategy prior to the War of 1812.[58]

The Jeffersonian military strategy proved "the military means did not equal the political goals of the United States."[59] This was the case during the War of 1812. The American military fell short of its political ambitions. The militia units normally did not have the same level of success on the battlefield against a disciplined military like the British. The militia units worked alongside the regular military. The "United States Constitution institutionalized the dual-army tradition,"[60] although the United States had some regular infantry, the militia units were the primary force for the American military.[61]

Coastal Fortifications

Coastal fortifications were another part of the American military strategy. Because of concerns with the British and other European powers, Congress voted to "rehabilitate coastal fortifications of the Revolutionary era."[62] Many of the coastal fortifications on the Great Lakes were small in comparison to ones along the Atlantic coast. These forts were garrisoned by small units with limited supplies. These forts were a "thin screen of stockade forts, most of which were also trading posts. Their tiny, sickly garrisons were merely symbols of the United States territorial claim to the Old Northwest."[63]

This also created a need for a naval force to aide in the protection of harbor ports and cities. As with all of Jefferson's policies, his idea of a navy included gunboats which were better for defensive activity, rather than offensive warfare. This strategy also caused problems for the American military during the War of 1812. All of these strategies show how the United States had a defensive mindset, but their political aspirations far exceeded its military's strength. Previous policies from past administrations created a military that was unprepared for war.

Military Technologies of the War of 1812

Military technology during the War of 1812 defined the tactics that were used on the battlefield. Weapons during this time were muskets, rifles, pistols, swords, pikes and a variety of different artilleries. These weapons came in a variety of forms. Both the British and American militaries used many different weapons for battle. Although the weapons fall into the same categories, they were designed for different reasons in battle. Details like caliber were different for both countries weapons.[64]

Both sides focused on gaining the edge on military technology. The British trained their soldiers to fire a musket at "two to three per minute."[65] The British used an "India Pattern musket with a 39 inch barrel which used a .71 caliber ball. The weight was around nine pounds. This musket had a 17 inch bayonet attached."[66] This musket was called the "Brown Bess."[67] The American military used a "Model 1795 Musket with a length of five feet which used a .65 caliber musket ball. The Model 1795 weighed around eleven pounds. It typically had a 15 inch bayonet on it."[68] Both weapons were effective at one hundred to about one hundred fifty yards but had a range of two hundred fifty yards.[69]

A second infantry weapon was the rifle. Rifles had a "spiral groove" within the barrel which made it more accurate than the musket's smooth barrel.[70] The British military used the Baker rifle which had a "30-30 ½ inch barrel. It used a .62 caliber weapon and had a bayonet of 23 inches."[71] The American military had two different rifles. The two styles were the "The Harper Ferry Model 1803 and the 1807 Pennsylvania Rifle."[72] Both styles of the America rifle "used a .54 caliber bullet and had a barrel of 33 inches. The American rifle was not designed for a bayonet."[73]

Other weapons used by infantry units during the War of 1812 were swords and pikes. Pikes had differing uses for the British and American militaries. The British used it primarily for sergeants and grenadier units. The British pike was "9 feet long with a 123/4 inch blade."[74] American militia used them however only one infantry unit used them. One third of the "15th Infantry, commanded by Colonel Zebulon M. Pike, used pikes.[75] Upon his death, the unit stopped using them. The American pike was typically "10 to 11 feet in length."[76] Swords on both sides were given to cavalry units. The British had specific swords which were based on rank. The British gave swords to artillery units. The American military gave all

Watt

"officers and non-commissioned officers" swords.[77]   Medical

personnel in the United States military were also given swords.[78]

Cavalry units used pistols alongside swords. The typical

British pistol "used a .66 caliber bullet. The two types of pistols

were the Elliott carbine and the Paget carbine. The difference was

the length of barrel. The barrel of the Elliott carbine was 28 inches

whereas the Paget carbine had a 16 inch barrel. The British also

gave the cavalry units a 33 inch sword."[79] The American military

gave cavalry units one of two pistols. The two pistols were the

"Model 1805 which had a .59 caliber or the Model 1811 which had a

.69 caliber."[80]

Other weapons used by both militaries during the War of

1812 were artillery. Artillery was categorized in three different

ways either for "field use, garrison (fort) use or for naval use."[81]

Artillery was based on the principle of loading gunpowder and a

form of projectile within the cannon which would fire in a variety of

ways. Artillery had different styles. The long gun was the most

popular artillery for the War of 1812. The long gun would fire a "6

pound cannon ball."[82] The Howitzer was a smaller but wider gun

that "fired exploding projectiles over obstacles."[83] The last type of

Watt

artillery was the Mortar. The Mortar would "fire projectiles in an

upward motion over forts and earthworks."[84] The British also used

a "Congreve Rocket."[85] This weapon fired a spear like projectile

over the enemy. It was not very effective except to scare untrained

or inexperienced military personnel.[86]

The War of 1812 saw a number of weapons used on both

sides. These weapons were used to expand the military's ability to

conquer the enemy. Victor Hanson discusses the importance that

technology played in western warfare. The War of 1812 was no

exception to this thinking. Both the British and Americans

attempted to control the battlefield through strategy and military

technology. Logistics played an important role with technology.

Many of the battles that are discussed show the importance logistics

on the battlefield.[87] See Appendix 3 for American weapons,

Appendix 4 for British weapons and Appendix 5 for Artillery

weapons.

Western Military Fortifications on the Great Lakes

The War of 1812 with Great Britain challenged American strategic policy. American political and military leaders understood the need to keep the Northwest Territory in American hands. The economic and strategic loss would be devastating to the United States. "On May 30, 1812, the Reporter Newspaper stated that Great Britain has commenced war in the western country, Northwest territory, equally as France would have done. The government must not abandon the western country to the British."[88] This is one example showing how important defending the Northwest Territory was to the citizens of the United States. Although there were a number of forts along the Great Lakes, the focus of this section will be based on the two strategic forts in Michigan, Fort Michilimackinac and Fort Detroit.[89]

The first Governor of the Michigan Territory, William Hull, saw the need to protect the Northwest Territory, as well as other American military leaders. One of his strategies was to reinforce the coastal fortifications along the Great Lakes. Manpower shortages prevented that from happening.[90] The Great Lakes fortifications did get some reinforcements, but logistical support was limited. They reinforced the idea that the United States held these fortifications in name only. These lightly staffed units were no match for the British military. This is what happened at Fort Michilimackinac.[91]

Fort Michilimackinac, otherwise known as Fort Mackinac, was "known as the Gibraltar of the Great Lakes."[92] Mackinac Island was called "Michilimackinac by the French and English."[93] The Island protected the Straits of Mackinac which connected Lake Michigan and Lake Huron at the northern tip of the Lower Peninsula of the Michigan Territory. The Straits of Mackinac were also called the "crossroads of the Great Lakes."[94] The Chippewa tribe called the island, "Michilimackinac," which is believed to be their word for "green turtle."[95] It was called "green turtle" because of it the "humped oval shape," which looked like a turtle coming out of Lake Huron which had plush green trees on it.[96] Americans would shorten "Michilimackinac to Mackinac."[97]

Initially, the French built Fort Michilimackinac (Mackinac), which was located on the northern coast of the Lower Peninsula of the Michigan Territory near the Straits of Mackinac. The British would gain control of it from the victory over France after the

French and Indian war. It would be moved to Mackinac Island by the British. This was because the Island was perfectly situated to be a good outpost for naval protection of the Great Lakes. Mackinac Island is a "three mile long and two mile wide" island located in Lake Huron near the Straits of Mackinac.[98] Fort Mackinac was a key port for fur trade. This had been a "hot spot with Canadian merchants."[99] This was because Americans would gain control from the British after the American Revolution. Attacking Fort Mackinac became an important strategic goal of the British military.[100]

The Battle of Fort Mackinac is known as the "bloodless victory."[101] The British would attack the fort during the night. They landed on the north side of the Island. The British marched straight through the middle of the Island behind Fort Mackinac. This was a good strategy because Fort Mackinac was high on the hillside and could easily attack incoming ships, and landing military forces in front of the fort. The weak spot was the rear but it was guarded by a dense forest and steep hillside. Another key factor was that Fort Mackinac was protected by a small American force of about "seventy-five men."[102] The commander for the American military at Fort Mackinac was Lieutenant Porter Hanks.[103]

Watt

On July 17, 1812 around 3 a.m., the British Commander, Captain Roberts, led the British forces through this dense forest in a straight line to the rear of the fort. Captain Robert's attack of Fort Mackinac was funded by the Canadian Northwest Fur Company who refitted shipped and gave supplies for the expedition. The British attacked with "forty-six regular infantry, one hundred fifty volunteers and four hundred Native Americans." Lieutenant Hanks heard of a British attack and sent men to investigate this information. Unfortunately for Hanks, his men were captured, and Captain Roberts took a position above Fort Mackinac behind the fort. He placed his only cannon towards it. The cannon had to be brought up by his men from the shore where they landed. The entire military force had to crawl up Mackinac Island's hilly center with the cannon.[104]

Captain Roberts sent word to Fort Mackinac's commander Lieutenant Hanks, asking for surrender or he would attack the fort. "Lieutenant Hanks surrendered without a fight. Lieutenant Hanks felt that the soldiers would be killed or murdered by the Native Americans. He believed that the killing of prisoners would again and again affect the outcome of future battles. Hanks understood

34

that this would increase the effectiveness of the British and Native American as allies and decrease Americans desire to fight."[105] This victory gave the British and opportunity to gain Native American allies in the entire Northwest Territory, including Michigan, because it now controlled an important port with its victory of Fort Mackinac.[106]

The British would control Fort Mackinac for the rest of the war. On August 4, 1814, the United States attempted an attack to regain Fort Mackinac. "Lieutenant Colonel George Crogham sails from Fort Detroit with seven hundred men to attack Michilimackinac (Mackinac)."[107] The goal of this attack was to regain Fort Mackinac and reduce the ability of the British to gain Native American allies. The American military did not realize that Lieutenant General Sir George Prevost had reinforced Fort Mackinac. This caused the attack to fail, and Lieutenant Colonel Crogham was forced to retreat. Unlike the American force that the British had beaten, the British reinforcements were well prepared for an attack on the island. Lieutenant Colonel Crogham left two ships, "the schooners Tigress and Scorpion to blockade Fort Mackinac" as he retreated back to Fort Detroit.[108]

During the retreat to Fort Detroit, Lieutenant Colonel Crogham found the "British ship Nancy hidden on the Nottawasaga River."[109] This ship was another property of the Northwest Fur Company who helped finance the war on the Great Lakes. This ship was the primary source of logistical supplies to Fort Mackinac. Lieutenant Colonel Crogham decided to capture or destroy the schooner Nancy. The British force on the Nancy was commanded by Lieutenant Miller Worsley. Instead of allowing the Americans to capture the Nancy, Lieutenant Worsley "set fire to the Nancy to prevent its capture."[110] Lieutenant Worsley took his force through the forest to avoid capture and found canoes to take him to Fort Mackinac. This act gave the American military the only ships on the Great Lakes. Lieutenant Worsley created a plan to take the two American ships that were blockading them.[111]

Lieutenant Worsley took several men and Native Americans to attack the Tigress. Although the Americans saw his men, he was still able to take the Tigress. Lieutenant Worsley then attacked the Scorpion by disguising it as an American ship. This allowed Lieutenant Worsley to get close to the Scorpion where he led a second attack. He easily captured both ships. This defeat would give the British the only naval ships on the Great Lakes. Lieutenant Colonel Crogham's victory was short lived and the British would keep the naval advantage on Lake Huron and Lake Michigan the rest of the war. Americans never attacked Fort Mackinac again, and the British held the fort until the end of the war.[112]

Days before the battle of Fort Detroit, was the battle of Brownstown. General Hull requested military supplies and reinforcements and were heading to Fort Detroit. At the same, time a British contingent was also heading towards Fort Detroit. The American Commander was Lieutenant Colonel Miller. The British was commanded by General Muir. The American military had fresh or green troops that had never seen battle, with a few exceptions who fought at the Battle of Tippecanoe. The British troops were well informed and hid in the brush and in the trees. The British ambushed the American forces and drew first blood with the death of an American soldier. Volleys from the American force attacked the British from both sides of the battlefield. This was the Kentucky militia that General Hull had requested. Because of the terrain and the inability of the British to form columns, the battle was in disarray. At that time the Native Americans attempted a flanking move, however, the Kentucky militia and other American units held the line and drove the Native Americans back into the trees. In the confusion of the battle, British forces fired and killed their own allies. Although the American forces won that day, they did not reach their final goal to reinforce Fort Detroit with fresh supplies.[113]

Fort Detroit was the nearest American fort in Michigan that could launch an attack on Canada. Fort Detroit was located north of Ohio, along the lower eastern coast in the Lower Peninsula of the Michigan Territory. The American forces, like Fort Mackinac, were under manned and short of supplies. This forced the commanders of Fort Detroit to declare Martial Law in order to procure supplies for their men. Part of this was because of the limited logistical support for the military in the Northwest Territory. General William Hull, Governor of the Michigan Territory, believed that Fort Detroit held the strategic position for the American military.[114]

The fall of Fort Mackinac created a bad situation for the initial invasion of Canada. General Hull's successes were nullified by this act and forced his retreat to Fort Detroit. This begins the first battle for Fort Detroit. General Hull requested reinforcements from the Kentucky militia and supplies for his military. General Hull knew that General Isaac Brock was heading towards Fort Detroit with a number of men. General Brock had also "intercepted communications between American officers and knew General Hull's desperate situation."[115] On August 15, 1812, the British would launch an invasion of the Michigan Territory against Fort Detroit.[116]

General Brock had approximately thirteen hundred men, including Native American warriors. General Hull had about twenty-two hundred regular infantry and militia soldiers; however, the Fort Detroit area had a civilian population too. General Brock landed near Fort Detroit along the Lake Erie shore. His military marched on Fort Detroit. General Brock initially requested Hull's immediate surrender prior to the attack but General Hull refused. The British launched a full scale attack and bombardment of the fort on the evening of August 15 and into August 16, which started taking a toll on the fort and the morale of the troops. General Hull wrote, "My God, what shall I do with all of these women and children?"[117] General Hull was concerned about the British allowing the Native Americans to murder innocent women and

Watt

children. General Hull eventually surrendered Fort Detroit to

General Brock.[118]

The loss of Fort Mackinac and Fort Detroit was devastating

to the United States and General Hull's mistakes and losses forced

American military leaders to appoint a new Commander of the

Northwest Army. General Hull would also face court martial

charges for his actions at Fort Detroit, which would take a

Presidential Pardon to protect him. This new officer was named

General William Benjamin Harrison, the territorial Governor of

Indiana. General Harrison's goals were to defeat the British at Fort

Detroit and launch a second invasion of Canada. General Harrison

also sent out "search and destroy missions" against Native American

tribes in the Ohio valley.[119] These events would force General

Harrison to send troops towards Detroit. Harrison would send

General Winchester to the Maumee River and eventually onto the

River Raisin.[120]

The Battle of River Raisin

Replica British cannon on a sled for snow travel
Picture taken by George P. Watt, Jr. at the River Raisin Battlefield in Monroe, Michigan
January 20, 2007.

The capture of Fort Detroit allowed the British to fight the American military at any given time. General Harrison, the new commander of the Northwest army, understood the British threat of invasion. He set up his army into "three columns."[121] Harrison sent the first column to Sandusky, Ohio. He sent the second column to the Maumee River, Ohio. The third column was sent to Fort Defiance, Ohio. General Winchester, in charge of the second

Watt

column was sent towards the Maumee River.[122] Harrison ordered

Winchester to avoid engaging the enemy on his way to the River

Raisin.[123]

Re-enactment of General Winchester at the Battle of River Raisin.
Picture taken by George P. Watt, Jr. at the River Raisin Battlefield, in Monroe,
Michigan January 20, 2007.

Dave Ingall, Assistant Director of the Monroe County

Historical Museum who runs the River Raisin Battlefield, gives an

account of General Winchester's route to Frenchtown.[124] Dave

Ingall states, "Winchester followed the same route that Anthony

Watt

Wayne, the Revolutionary War hero, followed to attack the British at

Fort Detroit." Ingall explains that "General Winchester started in

Cincinnati as one of General Harrison's three columns, the left wing.

General Harrison's army moved towards present day, Fort Wayne,

Indiana. Winchester was sent ahead by Harrison and came out west

of the Maumee River. Once at the Maumee River, Winchester

started heading toward Frenchtown."[125] Ingall explains that the river

was frozen over and there was about three feet of snow on the

ground which meant that the cannons were on sleds.[126] The Laurent

Dorocher diary adds credence to this battle as it describes the

"bloody events" that happened during the battle of River Raisin.[127]

Winchester heard the British were heading toward

Frenchtown. This put him very close to the British military and their

allies. "Harrison was still 60 miles away and because of this,

Winchester decided to act on his own and sent to word to Harrison."[128]

The road was tough because the brush was overgrown on the roads.

The Northwest did not have good roads to travel; all were overgrown

and surrounded by the dense forest with occasional open areas. The

entire territory was surrounded by wilderness which was conducive

to an ambush. This resulted in more time taken to prepare for a potential ambush. This slowed the troop movement. Part of Winchester's troops moved into Frenchtown on January 18, 1813.[129] After receiving correspondence from Winchester, "Harrison recognized Winchester's position and gathered a force of nine hundred men to relieve him."[130]

Day One - January 18, 1813

Frenchtown, which is modern day Monroe, Michigan, was a settlement inhabited primarily by French Americans and Native Americans, who made peace with the United States prior to the War of 1812. When Winchester's scouts arrived, they found a force of two hundred militia and four hundred Native Americans, allies of the British. Ralph Naveaux, an expert on the Battle of River Raisin, puts the numbers of the British forces at, "50 Essex Militia and a couple hundred Native Americans."[131] Winchester had sent

Re-enactment of the Battle of River Raisin January 20, 2007
Picture taken by George P. Watt, Jr. at the River Raisin Battlefield, in Monroe,
Michigan January 20, 2007.

one of his officers, Colonel Lewis, with five hundred and fifty men

to advance on Frenchtown. Naveaux would put the number of the

American force around "two hundred."[132] When Lewis arrived, he

assessed the situation and became confident in his numbers. Lewis

surprised the Canadian militia and won the battle. The Canadian

militia and Native American allies fled after the defeat.[133]

The Nile Weekly Register of Baltimore Maryland reports that

Colonel Lewis was very successful in his attempt to drive out the enemy in Frenchtown. Lewis's men defeated both Canadian militia and its Native American allies. Lewis's attack was around 3 a.m. on January 18, 1813, "the action lasted until night."[134] Native American casualties were heavy. American losses were ten dead and twelve wounded. General Winchester reinforced Frenchtown with an additional two hundred men bringing the total in River Raisin around a thousand men. The first day was a successful action against British forces.[135]

Day Two – January 22, 1813

"Despite warning from some locals, no extra precautions were taken to guard the American camp against a surprise attack from British forces."[136] Dave Ingall points out that Winchester's reinforcement bring the total around nine hundred thirty-four men. Ingall points out that this was both United Stated infantry units and Kentucky militia. Ingall explains that Winchester did not have defense set up and put his Headquarters nearly a mile away from his men. The British force under the command of General Proctor crossed the frozen river by foot, instead of crossing the river at the bridge several miles to the south. This created an element of surprise for the British.[137]

Watt

Around 5 a.m., the British attacked the American forces. The fighting started "below or easterly of Colonel Lewis's men."[138] This caused Lewis and his men to retreat over the River Raisin. He was putting his men in a position to retreat towards the Maumee River; however, most of the men that crossed the river were killed by Native Americans that attacked from all directions.[139] "Meanwhile on the American left about four hundred militia under the command of Major George Madison held off several attacks by the British military."[140]

Re-enactment of the Battle of River Raisin January 20, 2007
Picture taken by George P. Watt, Jr. at the River Raisin Battlefield, in Monroe,
Michigan January 20, 2007.

General Winchester was at his Headquarters when he heard

the fighting and took off by horse to lead his men. The action had

already been going on for a while by the time he got the battle.

"Outnumber and without Artillery, Winchester should have deployed

his men so that the River Raisin was to his front instead of his rear."[141]

He did attempt to rally his men but was captured during the battle.

The majority of the men were captured and taken to Fort Malden in

Canada because General Proctor feared an attack by General

Watt

Harrison. However, those that could not make the trip were left in

Frenchtown.[142] Major Madison refused to surrender, unless General

Proctor would agree that his men would be protected. General

Brock did not accept these terms; Major Madison explained that he

would fight to the death if needed. After hearing this, General

Brock agreed to protect Madison's militia; however, this request was

not fulfilled.[143]

Dave Ingall discusses how the Kentucky militia actually

fought better than the regular infantry during this battle. Typically,

regular infantry units were trained and better disciplined during

battles; however, the Kentucky militia soldiers were better than

typical militia units and performed well during the Battle of River

Raisin. Ingall points out that the Kentucky militia was winning the

battle when they were given news of Winchester's surrender. They

wanted to continue fighting; however, Winchester had surrendered

the entire military to General Proctor including the militia. This

bound them to complying with the surrender orders.[144]

General Winchester made several mistakes that cost him the

battle of River Raisin. The first mistake he made was not planning

for a British attack. The Nile Register writes that, "Winchester had not taken precautions of supplying his troops and they were scarcely able to fire five rounds."[145]   His second mistake was not sending out scouts to study the enemy's movements. His third mistake was not listening to the local civilians about a potential British attack. On the other hand, General Proctor took full advantage of not being detected by Winchester's men. His surprise attack was an exceptional military deployment; however, his actions after the battle are less than perfect.[146]

Day Three – January 23, 1813

By day three of the battle, the military engagement was over, however, there was still activity happening on the River Raisin. The Kentucky militia reported that General Proctor allowed his Native American allies to "attack and pillage the prisoners."[147] The British had promised to guard the prisoners that were left at Frenchtown, however, this never happened. On January 23, 1813, Native Americans came into the area that held the prisoners and began to set houses on fire and kill the prisoners. By the end of the day, all that had not escaped were killed. Approximately thirty-three prisoners escaped.[148] The killing went on for hours. Some were tomahawked or scalped, others just killed. General Proctor again was negligent in his duties to the prisoners. This is known as the Massacre on the Raisin. [149] See Appendix 1 for American losses & Appendix 2 for British losses for the Battle of River Raisin.

"The historical importance of the Battle of the River Raisin lies not merely in the battle itself, but also in the tragic aftermath. Winchester was certain he surrendered his force as prisoners of war, which entitled them to full British protection from the Indians. Testimony of other surviving Americans attested to their similar understanding."[150] General Proctor allowed the prisoners that were marched to Fort Malden, be mangled by his Native American allies. He also left eighty prisoners that were slaughtered at the River Raisin. In the end, only thirty-three would survive. Proctor's activities were an unusually cruel act from a British officer. This action would lead to the American slogan, "Remember the Raisin!"[151]

Michigan as a Focal Point for the Invasion of Canada

The invasion of Canada was not a new idea. Some American Revolutionary leaders had discussed this as a feasible idea. Prior to the War of 1812, political leaders had hoped to bring Canada into the United States. The first invasion of Canada would occur prior to the Battle of River Raisin. The second invasion of Canada would occur after the fall of Fort Detroit and the military loss at River Raisin. Unlike the United States, Great Britain had a vast amount of resources, although they too were becoming stretched with the Napoleonic wars. The lack of resources for the American military caused a lack of a real strategic policy with political and military leaders.[152]

Prior to the Battle of River Raisin, the first invasion of Canada was a direct result of American strategic goals. General Hull agreed and implemented this as part of his overall military strategy. Hull's strategy included taking the town of Sandwich, which he could use as his Canadian base of operation. The problems for the American military was the British military had three deployable naval ships, and had reinforced Upper Canada, which was the land around Lake Erie, Lake Ontario including York, which is modern day Toronto, with regular infantry. The British also had the luxury

Watt

of calling up local militia and Native American tribes to fight. The

American military did not have naval support and relied on keeping

a good supply chain back to Fort Detroit. On June 12, 1812, General

Hull invades Canada from Fort Detroit. Hull easily captured

Sandwich.[153]

After General Hull captured Sandwich, he attempted to

attack Fort Malden, which was south of Sandwich. Hull sent a force

to attack and during the march Native Americans allied to the British

attacked the American military. The attempted ambush failed to

defeat the American military, where four American soldiers were

killed, and the remaining Americans returned to Sandwich.

Instead, General Hull attempted to persuade Canadians to fight

against the British. Hull made a proclamation that allowed any

Canadian that aided American military efforts to keep and maintain

their property. When General Proctor heard of this, he created his

own proclamation, which reminded Canadians that their wealth was

a direct result of British military might.[154]

General Hull was given news of the American defeat at Fort

Mackinac. The fall of Fort Mackinac was a dual problem for the

Americans. It gave the British free access to create allies with new

Native American tribes throughout the Northwest Territory, which hindered General Hull's invasion of Canada. General Hull's situation worsened as he realized his supplies were running short. This led Hull to reassess his strategic situation. He decided to redeploy to Fort Detroit, ending the first invasion of Canada. General Hull would be blamed for his inaction against Fort Malden and his perceived retreat to Fort Detroit.[155] Prior to the first invasion of Canada and the Battle of River Raisin, Harrison wrote that, "American control of the Northwest depended on a successful naval campaign in 1813. The surrender of the American outpost at Mackinac and Detroit in July of 1812 had opened the entire Northwest frontier to enemy attack."[156]

General Harrison and the new Northwest army headed to attack Fort Detroit. General Hull had surrendered the entire first Northwest Army to General Proctor, when Hull lost Fort Detroit. Harrison's army had approximately seven thousand men. On September 27, 1813, Harrison and the American force are able to fortify and take the abandoned Fort Detroit. Retaking Fort Detroit opened the opportunity for a second invasion of Canada.[157] This was reinforced with naval Commander Oliver Hazard Perry's defeat of the British Navy at Put-In-Bay.[158] Harrison wrote to

Headquarters that, "as soon as I have driven the enemy from Malden

and Detroit, I shall dispatch a detachment for the retaking of

Mackinac and St. Joseph and will expect your orders for further

movements."[159]

General Harrison marched across Canada for a second

invasion. His goal was to defeat General Proctor's military and

chase him as far as he could. As Harrison's army marched on

Canada, Native American warriors allied to the British, attempted to

stop the American advance, however, they were driven back. The

American military continued to advance. "On October 5, 1813,

American forces captured two gunboats and soldiers who had been

left to guard them. These boats contained all the ammunition that

had not already been abandoned or issued to the British troops."[160]

The American military continued their pursuit of the British until

they were in sight.[161]

Near the Thames River, General Harrison initially decided to

attack the British with the regular infantry; however, the British were

in disarray and not in their normal tight formations. This allowed

Harrison to send Colonel Johnson's militia cavalry to charge into the

British lines. Johnson attacked yelling, "Remember the Raisin!"[162]

This forced the British to retreat in an abnormally disorganized way.

After defeating the British infantry, Johnson and his men attacked

the Native Americans by dismounting and engaging them. During

the Battle of Thames; Tecumseh, a Shawnee Chief, was killed, but

General Proctor escaped.[163]

General Harrison's next target was Montreal, however, this

would not happen; instead, American forces attacked York. "The

defeat of York was an embarrassment to the British; however, it was

not the decisive victory in the struggle to control Lake Ontario."[164]

The second Invasion of Canada was a success for the American

military. Although the United States never regained Fort Mackinac

or controlled Lake Ontario, it did conquer most of Upper Canada.

Because of capturing Upper Canada, the United States would control

part of the Great Lakes. It would take the Treaty of Ghent to reclaim

lost areas to the British. The American invasion proved the

importance of the Michigan territory as strategic position for the

American military.[165]

Analysis of Michigan's Role in the War of 1812

Watt

The thesis that the Michigan Territory was a vital area for the War of 1812, because of its location on the Great Lakes can be proven by analysis. Many factors explain the importance of Michigan's role during the War of 1812. The Northwest Territory saw a growth in American settlement and an increase in fur trade, both of these became concerns of the Native American tribes. The Shawnee Chief, Tecumseh, attempted to reunite all the tribes against the United States. As the War of 1812 began, this anti-American talk from Native Americans played right into the British military strategy. The British would use any means to destroy the United States.[166]

In the introduction, a series of questions were asked that need to be addressed. The first question, can it be proven that Michigan played a significant role in the War of 1812? The answer is yes, Michigan's strategic location on the Great Lakes was a perfect target for the British. American letters from military and political leaders explain the importance of the Northwest Territory. These leaders understood how important it was to keep the Michigan Territory out of British hands. They saw the British would have an opportunity to attack the United States from the north if they controlled the

Michigan Territory. American military leaders aggressively pursued, capturing lost territory. Fort Detroit in the Michigan Territory was controlled by the American and British militaries during the War of 1812, both understood the importance of this fort, as being a means of waging war against each other.[167]

The second question, why was the Michigan Territory so important to the United States and Great Britain? The answer to this question has two parts. First is the importance of the fur trade. In the 18th and early 19th centuries, the Michigan Territory was one of the important areas for the fur trade. This has significant proof because the French, British and United States all had troops protecting the Michilimackinac (Mackinac) areas. Another key fact is the Northwest Fur Trading Company had funded the British attack on Fort Mackinac. The second point is the Michigan Territory was the focal point for attacks by the British and American militaries. The British saw that controlling the Michigan Territory would allow them to attack the United States Army from multiple fronts. The American military saw the Michigan Territory as an opportunity for one side of an attack on Canada.[168]

The third question, were there any major battles in Michigan? The only major battle to occur in the Michigan Territory was the Battle of River Raisin. The River Raisin was a battle that played a key role in the War of 1812, which would inspire the American military to fight. Dave Ingall reaffirms that the River Raisin was the only major battle that took place within Michigan. Ingall also reaffirms the significance of the fighting in Frenchtown. Ingall's explains how day three of the Battle of River Raisin inspired the American military because it was seen as a massacre on American lives.[169]

Additionally, the massacre on day three can also be evaluated from another perspective. Dave Ingall discusses some reasons why the massacre occurred. He explains that it was true that General Proctor did not restrain his Native American allies, which was one of many issues. The Native Americans fighting in this battle had a grudge against both the Kentucky militia going back to the days of Daniel Boone and American settlers on their land. Another explanation can be from the missions that General Harrison had sent to destroy Native American settlements. He reaffirms that regardless of the grudge, Proctor handled the prisoners poorly.[170]

Watt

The River Raisin had another significant point. The battle itself started with an American victory, but ended with a British victory. The key to this battle was the day three massacre that occurred to the prisoners that were left at Frenchtown. This ignited a rallying cry that inspired the American military for the remaining time of the war. Karl Keisler writes, "All over America people were made sad by the tragedy at Frenchtown and the defeat of the Americans. 'Remember the Raisin' became the battle cry of the War of 1812."[171] Keisler explains the "Remember the Raisin" rallying cry was equal to "Remember Maine" during the Spanish American war.[172]

The fourth question, did an invasion occur from any part of Michigan into Canada? An invasion of Canada was an important goal for the United States. The invasion would take place from New York and the Michigan Territory. Fort Detroit was the key to this invasion. As the Americans held Fort Detroit, it was able to invade Canada; however, when the British held the fort, it could launch attacks into the United States. The Michigan Territory became the door for each army to invade the enemy's country.[173]

Watt

The fifth question, how did the British take the coastal fortifications in the Michigan Territory so easily? The British easily took fortifications from the United States and Fort Mackinac is an example of this. The strength of the British military, lack of supplies and the depleted American military units were the primary reasons why they so easily took the fortifications in the beginning of the war. Unfortunately, the United States was not prepared for war, and the coastal fortifications on the Great Lakes are an example of this. The American military had a presence on these forts, but were very small in comparison to the British units attacking them.[174]

The final question, was Fort Michilimackinac and Fort Mackinac the same fort? Fort Michilimackinac and Fort Mackinac is the same fort; however, the position of the fort changed throughout the years. The French were the first to settle and Michilimackinac became a thriving center for fur trade. As the French lost the French and Indian War, it surrendered the territory to Great Britain. The British would move the fort to Mackinac Island. After the American Revolution, Great Britain would give Fort Mackinac to the United States.[175]

The Treaty of Ghent would end the War of 1812. It also forced each country to return conquered territories to the original country. Who won the war? The British believed they had won. The British did not have to admit to impressing sailors or blockading American ports. The Canadians believed they had won because the United States fell short of conquering Canada. The United States felt they won because of the military successes that occurred; given lost territory back. The United States earned global respect from this war. In the end, each country has a claim to victory, but the last part on global respect gives the United States the key to claiming victory in the War of 1812.[176]

Donald R. Hickey disputes American's claim as to why it declared war on Great Britain with his "cost of doing business in a war torn world theory."[177] This idea is plausible but lacks an understanding of American political and strategic goals. Equally important is how unprepared the American military was to meet the ambition of its political leaders. The cost of doing business is an unacceptable reasoning for any neutral country to endure. The bigger issue was that America became a financial power in the world. The military of the United States was not in a position to aide

Watt

American merchants by protecting them against British

impressments and privateering.[178]

Watt

Conclusion

67

In conclusion, the Michigan Territory was a key area for both the American and British militaries. The Michigan Territory would see a number of battles. Each of these battles played a role in the balance of power for each military. Both countries gained and lost territories to the other. Although both retained its previously owned territory, the United States would benefit from the recognition of winning the War of 1812. The financial growth of the United States would force American leaders to rethink its military strategy. It would set the stage for the shift in American military thinking and world politics.

The most significant battle in the Michigan Territory was in Frenchtown. The Battle of River Raisin inspired the United States to rally and retake lost territories. It also reinvigorated a second invasion of Canada. Although American military leaders made mistakes at the River Raisin, it was the events after the fighting that would inspire future battles. This massacre would not be forgotten, and would be heard on the battlefield the remainder of the war. In the end, the battle would inspire the United States citizens and military to "Remember the Raisin!"

Appendix

Appendix 1 – American Losses at the River Raisin*[179]

American Killed	
Staff Officers	2
17th US Infantry	15
19th US Infantry	Unknown
1st Kentucky Militia	5
5th Kentucky Rifle	22
1st Kentucky Rifle	50
Volunteer Dragoons	3
Local Militia	4
Unaccounted or Missing	300

* Only 33 prisoners escaped.[180]

Appendix 2 – British Losses at the River Raisin[181]

British Killed		British Wounded	
41st Foot	15	41st Foot	106
Royal Artillery	2	Royal Artillery	8
10th Royal Battalion	0	10th Royal Battalion	2
Royal Newfoundland	2	Royal Newfoundland	2
Provincial Marines	1	Provincial Marines	26
1st Essex Militia	4	1st Essex Militia	0
2nd Essex Militia	3	2nd Essex Militia	0
Native Americans	25	Native Americans	0

Watt

Appendix 3 – American Weapons during the War of 1812[182]

American Weapons			
Weapons	Comments	Length	Caliber (if a gun)
Model 1795 Musket	11 pounds and had a 15 inch bayonet	Barrel - 5 feet	.65
Harper Ferry Model 1803 Rifle	No bayonet	Barrel - 33 inches	.54
1807 Pennsylvania Rifle	No bayonet	Barrel - 33 inches	.54
American Pike		10-11 feet	Not applicable
Model 1805 Pistol		Barrel – 10-12 inches	.59
Model 1811 Pistol		Barrel – 18 ½ inches	.69
Swords	Given to a number of units	Varied	Not applicable

Appendix 4 – British Weapons during the War of 1812[183]

British Weapons			
Weapons	Comments	Length	Caliber (if a gun)
Brown Bess	9 pounds with a 17 inch bayonet	Barrel - 39 inches	.71
Baker Rifle	Had a 23 inch bayonet	30-30 1/2 inch barrel	.62
British Pike	123 ½ blade	9 feet long	Not applicable
Elliot Carbine Pistol		Barrel - 28 inches	.66
Paget Pistol		Barrel - 16 inches	.66
Swords		Varied	Not applicable

Appendix 5 – Artillery during the War of 1812[184]

Artillery Weapons	
The Long Gun	Fired 6 pound cannon balls
Howitzer	Fired projects over enemy
Mortar	Fired over fort walls and earthworks

End Notes

[1] Alec R. Gilpin, *The War of 1812 in the Old Northwest,* (East Lansing: The Michigan State University Press: 1958), 24.

[2] Gilpin, 26.

[3] Gilpin, 3-226.

[4] Ibid, 23.

[5] Ibid, 28.

[6] Allan R. Millett and Peter Maslowski, *For the Common Defense: A Military History of the United States of America,* (New York: The Free Press: 1994), 93.

[7] Russell F. Weigley, The American Way of War: A History of United States Military Strategy and Policy, (Bloomington: Indiana University Press: 19770, 3-477.

[8] John Lynn, *Battle: A History of Combat and Culture,* (Cambridge: Westview Press: 2003), 1-369.

[9] Battle of Frenchtown—Massacre of River Raisin: An account of the Role of Monroe in the War of 1812 as Written by an Eye-witness Inhabitant. Monroe County Historical Archives: Michigan Military History – War of 1812 - Civil War – WWI. March 10, 2007.

[10] Donald R. Hickey, *The War of 1812: A Short History,* (Chicago: Illini Books: 1995), 1-120.

[11] Hickey, 41.

[12] Pierre Berton, *The Invasion of Canada 1812-1813,* (Boston: Little, Brown and Co.: 1980), 101-279.

[13] Wesley B. Turner, *"The War of 1812: The War that Both Sides Won,* (Toronto: The Dungurn Group: 2000), 30-131.

[14] Victor Davis Scott, *Carnage and Culture,* (New York: Anchor Books: 2002), 1-486.

[15] Hanson, 13.

[16] Ibid, 21.

[17] Ibid, 21.

[18] Ibid, 1-486.

[19] Ibid, 1-486.

[20] Donald R Hickey, *Don't Give Up the Ship! Myths of the War of 1812,* (Chicago: University of Illinois Press: 2006), 1-368.

[21] Hickey, 21.

[22] Ibid, 23.

[23] Ibid, 1-368.

[24] Ibid, 20.

[25] Ibid, 21.

[26] Ibid, 1-368.

[27] Ibid, 21.

[28] Ibid, 1-368.

[29] Ibid, 1-368.

[30] Ibid, 1-368.

[31] Ibid, 228.

[32] Ibid, 1-368.

[33] Hagan, Kenneth I. *The People's Navy: The Making of American Sea Power,* (New York: The Free Press: 1991), 1-390.

[34] Hickey, 1-368.

[35] Ibid, 1-1368.

[36] Donald R. Hickey, *The War of 1812: A Forgotten Conflict*, (Chicago: University of Illinois Press: 1989), 183.

[37] Ibid, 5-322.

[38] Benson J. Lossing, *Lossings's Pictorial Field Book of War of 1812 Volume 1,* (Grentna: A Firebird Press Book: 2003), 271.

[39] Benton, 3-131.

[40] Ibid, 159.

[41] Ibid, 159.

[42] Weigley, 49.

[43] Hagan, 63.

[44] Ibid, 1-390.

[45] Benson J. Lossing, *Lossings's Pictorial Field Book of War of 1812 Volume 1,* (Grentna: A Firebird Press Book: 2003), 667.

[46] Ibid, 1-390.

[47] Wiegley, 45.

[48] Ibid, 46.

[49] Ibid, 3-477.

[50] Hickey, *Don't Give Up the Ship,* 1-368.

[51] George Rogers Taylor, *The War of 1812: Past Justifications and Present Interpretations*, Lexington: D. C. Heath and Company: 1963), 43.

[52] Berton, 30-131.

[53] John Grenier, *The First Way of War: American War Making on the Frontier,* (Cambridge: Cambridge University Press: 2005), 1-225.

[54] Grenier, 207-210.

[55] Ibid, 1-225.

[56] Ibid, 1-225.

[57] David S. Heidler and Jeanne T. Heidler, *The War of 1812,* (Westport: Greenwood Press: 2002), 56.

[58] Weigley, 3-477.

[59] Ibid, 45.

[60] Millett, 93.

[61] Ibid, 1-654.

[62] Weigley, 42.

[63] John R. Elting, *Amateurs, To Arms! A Military History Of The War Of 1812,* (Chapel Hill: Da Capo Press: 1995), 23.

[64] Turner, 133-137.

[65] Hickey, *Don't Give Up the Ship*, 238.

[66] Turner, 133-134.

[67] Hickey, 238.

[68] Ibid, 133.
[69] Ibid, 133-137.
[70] Ibid, 134.
[71] Ibid, 134.
[72] Hickey, 241.
[73] Turner, 134.
[74] Ibid, 134.
[75] Ibid, 134.
[76] Ibid, 134.
[77] Ibid, 134.
[78] Ibid, 133-137.
[79] Ibid, 135.
[80] Ibid, 135.
[81] Hickey, 230.
[82] Turner, 135.
[83] Ibid, 135.
[84] Ibid, 135.
[85] Hickey, 236.
[86] Ibid, 236-238.
[87] Hanson, 1-463.
[88] Taylor, 43.
[89] Ibid, 1-114.
[90] Gilpin, 3-226.
[91] Elting, 1-339.
[92] Francis F. Beirne, *The War of 1812,* (Hamden: Archon Books: 1965), 103.
[93] Walter R. Borneman, *The War of 1812: The War That Forged a Nation,* (New York: Perennial: 2004), 63.
[94] Borneman, 63.
[95] Ibid, 63.
[96] Ibid, 63.
[97] Ibid, 63.
[98] Ibid, 63.
[99] Reginald Horseman, *The War of 1812,* (New York: Alfred A. Knopf: 1969), 36.
[100] Horseman, 2-102.
[101] Benton, 101.
[102] A. J. Langguth, *Union 1812: The Americans Who Fought the Second War of Independence,* (New York: Simon & Schuster: 2006), 182.
[103] Turner, 40.
[104] Ibid, 40.
[105] Ibid, 40.
[106] Ibid, 6-149.
[107] Ibid, 102.
[108] Ibid, 102.
[109] Ibid, 102.

[110] Ibid, 102.

[111] Ibid, 6-149.

[112] Ibid, 6-149.

[113] Berton, 158-163.

[114] Horseman, 2-102.

[115] Gilpin, 115.

[116] Ibid, 3-226.

[117] Berton, 179.

[118] Carl Benn, *The War of 1812,* (New York: Osprey Publishing: 2002), 7-90.

[119] Berton, 279.

[120] Horsman, 2-102.

[121] Beine, 141.

[122] Ibid, 141.

[123] Ibid, 141.

[124] Dave Ingall, Assistant Director Monroe County Historical Museum. 126 S. Monroe, Street, Monroe, Michigan 48161. Interviewed Saturday January 20, 2007.

[125] Ingall Interview.

[126] Ibid.

[127] *Laurent Durocher's Account of the River Raisin: January 18, 22, & 23, 1813.* Monroe County Historical Archives: Michigan Military History – War of 1812 Civil War – WWI. March 10, 2007.

[128] Beirne, 144.

[129] Ibid, 102-144.

[130] Ibid, 145.

[131] Ralph Naveaux, *Blood On The Raisin: The Story of the Battles and Massacre of the River Raisin.* Monroe County Historical Archives: Michigan Military History - War of 1812 - Civil War – WWI. March 10, 2007.

[132] Naveaux, *Blood On The Raisin.*

[133] Beine, 102-144.

[134] *The Battle of the River Raisin (Battle of Frenchtown): Excerpts form the Niles Weekly Registrar Baltimore February 13, 1813, March 6 1813, April 10, 1813.* Monroe County Historical Archives: Michigan Military History – War of 1812 – Civil War – WWI. March 10, 2007.

[135] Nile Weekly Register.

[136] Naveaux, *Blood On The Raisin.*

[137] Ingall Interview.

[138] Naveaux, *Blood On The Raisin.*

[139] *Laurent Durocher's Account of the River Raisin*

[140] Harry L. Coles, *The War of 1812,* (Chicago: The University of Chicago Press: 1965), 116.

[141] Ibid, 116.

[142] *Laurent Durocher's Account of the River Raisin.*

[143] Coles, 115-136.

[144] Ingall Interview.

[145] The Nile Weekly Register.

[146] Beirne, 103-144.

[147] Naveaux, *Blood On The Raisin.*

[148] Ingall Interview.

[149] Naveaux, *Blood On The Raisin.*

[150] Gilpin, 170.

[151] Ibid, 170.

[152] Hagan, 1-390.

[153] Gilpin, 3-226.

[154] Ibid, 3-226.

[155] Ibid, 3-226.

[156] William S. Dudley (Ed), *The Naval War of 1812: A Documented History Volume II,* (Washington DC: Naval Historical Center Department of Navy: 1992), 417.

[157] Ibid, 2-326.

[158] Benn, 46.

[159] Dudley, 566.

[160] Cole, 132.

[161] Coles, 115-136.

[162] Hickey, *The War of 1812: A short story,* 41.

[163] Coles, 115-136.

[164] Horsman, 94.

[165] Ibid, 115-136.

[166] Hickey, *The War of 1812: The Forgotten Conflict,* 5-322.

[167] Gilpin, 3-226.

[168] Ibid, 3-226.

[169] Ingall Interview.

[170] Ingall Interview.

[171] Karl Zeisler, *A Brief History of Monroe,* (Monroe: Monroe Evening News: 1969), 19.

[172] Ibid, 19.

[173] Berton, 101-307.

[174] Turner, 6-149.

[175] Borneman, 1-304.

[176] Turner, 131.

[177] Hickey, 1-368.

[178] Ibid, 5-322.

[179] American Dead and Wounded at the Battle of the River Raisin, (http://www.co.monroe.mi.us/default.aspx?PageID=279).

[180] Ingall Interview.

[181] British Dead and Wounded at the Battle of the River Raisin, (http://www.co.monroe.mi.us/default.aspx?PageID=278).

[182] Turner, 133-134.

[183] Ibid, 133-134.

[184] Ibid, 133-134.

Bibliography

Primary Sources

Battle of Frenchtown—Massacre of River Raisin: An account of the Role of Monroe in
    the War of 1812 as Written by an Eye-witness Inhabitant. Monroe County
    Historical Archives: Michigan Military History – War of 1812 - Civil War –
    WWI. Copied March 10, 2007.

Ingall, Dave, Assistant Director Monroe County Historical Museum. 2007. 126 S.
    Monroe Street, Monroe, Michigan 48161. Interviewed Saturday January 20.

Laurent Durocher's Account of the River Raisin: January 18, 22, & 23, 1813.
    Monroe County Historical Archives: Michigan Military History – War of 1812 -
    Civil War – WWI. Copied March 10, 2007.

Naveaux, Ralph, *Blood On The Raisin: The Story of the Battles and Massacre of the*
    River Raisin. Monroe County Historical Archives: Michigan Military History –
    War of 1812 - Civil War – WWI. Copied March 10, 2007.

The Battle of the River Raisin (Battle of Frenchtown): Excerpts from the Niles Weekly
    Registrar Baltimore February 13, 1813, March 6 1813, April 10, 1813. Monroe
    County Historical Archives: Michigan Military History – War of 1812 - Civil
    War – WWI. Copied March 10, 2007.

Secondary Sources

American Dead and Wounded at the Battle of the River Raisin.
    http://www.co.monroe.mi.us/default.aspx?PageID=279.
Cited December
    18, 2006.

Beirne, Francis F. 1965. *The War of 1812*. Hamden: Archon Press.

Benn, Carl. 2002. *The War of 1812*. University Park: Osprey
Publishing.

Berton, Pierre. 1980. *The Invasion of Canada: 1812-1813*.
Boston: Little, Brown and
    Company.

British Dead and Wounded at the Battle of the River Raisin.
    http://www.co.monroe.mi.us/default.aspx?PageID=278.
Cited December
    18, 2006.

Borneman, Walter R. 2004. *1812: The War That Forged A Nation*,
New York:
    Perennial.

Coles, Harry L. 1965. *The War of 1812*. Chicago: The University
of Chicago Press.

Dudley, William S. 1992. *The Naval War of 1812: A Documentary
History Volume II*.
    Washington D.C: Naval Historical Center Department of
Navy.

Elting, John R. 1995. *Amateurs, To Arms! A Military History Of
The War Of 1812*.
    Chapel Hill: Da Capo Press.

Gilpin, Alec R. 1958. *The War of 1812 in the Old Northwest*. East

Lansing: The
        Michigan State University Press.

Grenier, John. 2005. *The First Way of War: American War Making on the Frontier.*
        Cambridge: Cambridge University Press.

Hagan, Kenneth I. 1991. *The People's Navy: The Making of American Sea Power.*
        New York: The Free Press.

Hanson, Victor Davis. 2002. *Carnage and Culture.* Anchor Books: New York

Heidler, David S. and Jeanne T. Heidler. 1955. *The War of 1812.* Westport:
        Greenwood Press.

Hickey, Donald R. 2006. *Don't Give UP the Ship! Myths of the War of 1812.*
        Cambridge: University of Illinois Press.

Hickey, Donald R. 1989. *The War of 1812: A Forgotten Conflict.* Chicago: University
        of Illinois Press.

Hickey, Donald R. 1995. *The War of 1812: A Short History.* Chicago: University of
        Illinois Press.

Horseman, Reginald. 1969. *The War of 1812.* New York: Alfred A Knopf.

Langgnuth, A. J. 2006. *Union 1812: The Americas Who Fought The Second War of
        Independence.* New York: Simon & Schuster.

Lossing, Benson J. 2003. *Lossings's Pictorial Field Book of War of*

1812 Volume I.
        Grentna: A Firebird Press Book.

Lossing, Benson J. 2003. *Lossings's Pictorial Field Book of War of 1812 Volume 2.*
        Grentna: A Firebird Press Book.

Lynn, John A. 2003. *Battle: A History of Combat and Culture.* Cambridge: Westview
        Press.

Mahon, John K. 1972. *The War of 1812.* Gainesville: Da Capo Press.

Millett, Allan R. and Peter Maslowski. 1994. *For the Common Defense: A Military*
        History of the United States of America. New York: The Free Press.

River Raisin Battlefield.
http://www.co.monroe.mi.us/default.aspx?PageID=49.
        Cited December 18, 2006.

Taylor, George Rogers. 1963. *The War of 1812: Past Justifications and Present*
        Interpretations. Lexington: D. C. Heath and Company.

Turner, Wesley B. 2000. *The War of 1812: The War That Both Sides Won Second*
        Edition. Toronto: The Dundurn Group.

Weigley, Russell F. 1977. *The American Way of War: A History of United States*
        Military Strategy and Policy. Bloomington: Indiana University Press.

Zeisler, Karl. 1969. *A Brief History of Monroe.* Monroe: Monroe Evening News.

Made in the USA
Columbia, SC
08 April 2019